A MONARCH *in the* MAKING

From Accession to Coronation

The Official Coronation Souvenir

✠ Contents

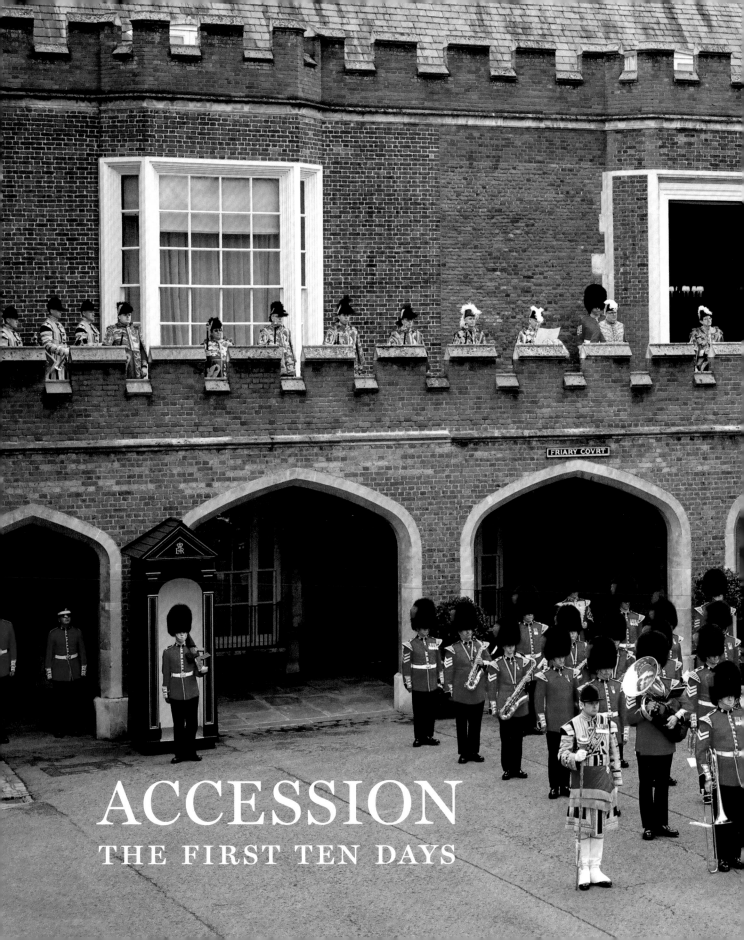

ACCESSION
THE FIRST TEN DAYS

The Accession of King Charles III, 8 September 2022

THE DEATH OF QUEEN ELIZABETH II on 8 September 2022 was a sad day for the nation and the Commonwealth, setting in train a period of mourning and culminating in her State Funeral on 19 September. But it also triggered a series of important constitutional events as the Crown passed down the line of succession to her eldest son. This book illustrates and explains the many steps that had to be taken to transform the reign of Queen Elizabeth II into the reign of King Charles III. The rules governing the Accession are enshrined in the Act of Succession of 1701. This sets out the conditions that must be satisfied if the heir to the throne is to be crowned, and the limits to his or her powers.

For a monarch is made by more than inheritance. The United Kingdom is a constitutional monarchy, in which the Sovereign is Head of State, but the ability to make and pass legislation resides with an elected Parliament. King Charles III's role as Sovereign had to be confirmed by a number of formalities and ceremonial steps of great legal and constitutional significance. The Coronation on 6 May 2023 marked the culmination of this process.

Even so, the months leading up to the Coronation were not lacking in the pomp and ceremony that signal a new reign. In the days that followed his Accession, at a time of national and personal mourning, The King embarked on an intensive itinerary that combined his constitutional and symbolic duties with reassurance about the continuity of the monarchy at a time of profound change for the country. The following months were a time of 'firsts' for the new King, taking part in State occasions and visiting regions of the country as he had done many times as Prince of Wales, but now for the first time as our monarch.

The King's First Address to the Nation, 9 September 2022

EVER SINCE THE INVENTION of radio enabled monarchs to speak directly to the nation, an address by the Sovereign has played a key role in unifying people across the country at times both of crisis and of celebration.

The announcement of Queen Elizabeth II's death on Thursday 8 September 2022 led to an outpouring of emotion around the UK and tributes from around the world. One of King Charles III's first public acts as monarch was therefore to express the sorrow of the nation the following day. In a broadcast from Buckingham Palace, The King acknowledged that the sadness felt by so many echoed the private grief of the Royal Family. He paid tribute to Her late Majesty and to the 'profound personal commitment which defined her whole life'. He talked about the duties of a Sovereign, pledging himself to uphold the constitutional principles at the heart of the nation, and promising that 'wherever you may live in the United Kingdom, or in the Realms and territories across the world, and whatever may be your background or beliefs, I shall endeavour to serve you with loyalty, respect and love, as I have throughout my life'.

In an address watched by millions around the world, The King spoke with affection of his wife, Camilla, and of his sons, William and Harry. He confirmed that William, who had automatically become Duke of Cornwall when his father acceded to the throne, was now also created Prince of Wales, a title held by The King himself for more than 64 years.

The King thanked his late mother 'for your love and devotion to our family and to the family of nations you have served so diligently all these years'. He closed his address with the moving wish that 'flights of Angels sing thee to thy rest', quoting the words spoken by Horatio at the death of his friend Hamlet, Prince of Denmark.

Seated at his desk in Buckingham Palace, King Charles III spoke for a nation in mourning when he described his mother's reign as 'a life well lived'.

The Accession Council and Principal Proclamation, 10 September 2022

T HE FIRST OFFICIAL EVENT of King Charles III's reign took place on Saturday 10 September 2022 when the Accession Council, a ceremonial body composed of Privy Councillors, was summoned to St James's Palace.

The role of the Accession Council is to recognise formally the death of one sovereign and confirm the accession of another. A proclamation was issued, the wording dictated by historical convention: 'with one voice and Consent of Tongue and Heart' the Council recognised that King Charles III was now King, Head of the Commonwealth and Defender of the Faith. A pledge of loyalty was read aloud and signed by the Prime Minister, the Archbishop of Canterbury and the Lord Chancellor, the archaic phrasing and rituals disguising the fact that the Proclamation of the Accession Council is not a quaint tradition but a legal and ceremonial requirement underpinning the principles of a constitutional monarchy and confirming King Charles III as Sovereign.

The Proclamation was announced to the public with a fanfare of trumpets and read out in Friary Court at St James's Palace, as is traditional, by Garter King of Arms, the senior herald at the College of Arms, who is known as Garter (after the Order of the Garter). The ceremony concluded when Garter proclaimed 'Three Cheers for His Majesty The King'; the soldiers in the courtyard below removed their bearskins to respond 'hip, hip, hurrah' and the national anthem was played by the trumpeters and the Band of the Coldstream Guards. Members of the public watching joined in, the first time the words 'God Save The King' had been sung since King George VI was on the throne, more than 70 years previously.

In the days before instant communication, the news that a monarch had died and another had acceded to the throne was spread throughout the kingdom by sending copies of the Principal Proclamation to be read out in towns and cities across the land. This tradition continues, even though the Accession ceremony was broadcast to the world for the first time in history.

OPPOSITE:
As the Principal Proclamation of the new King took place at St James's Palace (above), a 62-gun salute was fired from Tower Wharf at the Tower of London by the Honourable Artillery Company, the oldest regiment in the British Army (below).

Proclamations across the United Kingdom, 10 and 11 September 2022

T HE PRINCIPAL PROCLAMATION at St James's Palace on 10 September was followed by a second, read out at noon, at the Royal Exchange in the City of London, historically the financial and trade hub of the country and the centre of communication. The pageantry that accompanied the reading of the Proclamation in London was replicated in ceremonies that took place the following day in Scotland, Northern Ireland and Wales, in towns and cities across the UK and in Commonwealth countries where King Charles III was acclaimed as the new Head of State.

At Mercat Cross, next to St Giles' Cathedral, in Edinburgh, where Queen Elizabeth II was later to lie at rest for 24 hours, Lord Lyon King of Arms, the chief heraldic officer of Scotland, read out the Proclamation to that nation. The ceremony was introduced by a fanfare of trumpets and followed by a 21-gun salute at Edinburgh Castle. The party then processed to the castle where the Proclamation was made a second time on the castle drawbridge.

At exactly the same time, the Proclamation was read to the people of Northern Ireland at Hillsborough Castle, the Royal Family's official residence. The ceremony began with the Royal Irish Regiment leading a procession of a Proclamation Guard to the front of the castle. A fanfare was sounded by a bugler and a bell in the clock tower of the castle's Court House chimed once at noon precisely to signal the start of the reading of the Proclamation by the senior heraldic officer in Northern Ireland, known as Norroy and Ulster King of Arms.

In the Welsh capital, a Proclamation Guard from the Royal Welsh Regiment marched with the regimental band and mascot from City Hall to Cardiff Castle, where the Proclamation was read in English and then in Welsh. The reading was followed by a 21-gun salute and the singing of 'God Save The King' and the Welsh national anthem, 'Hen Wlad Fy Nhadau' ('Land of my Fathers').

The Ceremony of the Keys, Palace of Holyroodhouse, 12 September 2022

A S THE SUCCESSION WAS PROCLAIMED around the country, and The King began his first constitutional duties, the long-established plans made in the event of Queen Elizabeth II's death, code-named 'Operation London Bridge', began to unfold. Because the Queen died at Balmoral Castle, special arrangements were put in place to bring the coffin back to London from Scotland. This was known as 'Operation Unicorn' after Scotland's heraldic symbol.

Draped in the Royal Standard of Scotland, also known as the 'Lion Rampant', the oak coffin was topped with a wreath made from dahlias, sweet peas, phlox, white heather and pine fir. It was carried to the waiting hearse from the Castle's ballroom by six gamekeepers (known as ghillies in Scotland) from the Balmoral estate. On Sunday 11 September, the cortège made its way to Edinburgh, the long journey flanked by Scots paying tribute to Her late Majesty.

After its 180-mile journey, the coffin finally arrived at the Palace of Holyroodhouse, the Sovereign's official residence in Scotland, and was carried to rest in the Throne Room, where palace staff were able to pay their respects.

Accompanied by The Queen, King Charles III flew from London the following morning and inspected a Guard of Honour in the forecourt of Holyroodhouse before taking part for the first time as monarch in the Ceremony of the Keys. Welcoming The King to 'your ancient and hereditary kingdom of Scotland', the Lord Provost of Edinburgh offered the keys to the city of Edinburgh, which The King duly returned with the words: 'I return these keys, being perfectly convinced that they cannot be placed in better hands than those of the Lord Provost and Councillors of my good City of Edinburgh'.

ABOVE:
Queen Elizabeth II's coffin leaves Balmoral Castle for Edinburgh.

OPPOSITE:
The King inspects the Guard of Honour during the Ceremony of the Keys.

Edinburgh ceremonies,
12 and 13 September 2022

T HE CEREMONY OF THE KEYS was only the first event of the day for The King and Queen. Accompanied by The Princess Royal, The Duke of York and The Earl of Wessex (now The Duke of Edinburgh), The King led the procession of Queen Elizabeth II's coffin from the Palace of Holyroodhouse to its place of rest in St Giles' Cathedral. The procession was escorted by the Royal Company of Archers, who form the Sovereign's Bodyguard in Scotland, a function performed by the Yeomen of the Guard and the Gentlemen of Arms in other parts of the kingdom.

At St Giles' Cathedral, The King and Queen and other members of the Royal Family attended a Service of Thanksgiving for the life of Her late Majesty.

After receiving a motion of condolence at the Scottish Parliament Building and attending a reception there with The Queen, The King then held a vigil at St Giles' Cathedral with his sister and two brothers. The coffin lay at rest in the cathedral for 24 hours, during which time more than 26,000 mourners queued for up to 12 hours to view the late Queen's coffin and pay their final respects.

Northern Ireland welcomes The King and Queen, 13 September 2022

ABOVE:
The King and Queen enjoy meeting
well-wishers in Belfast.

OPPOSITE:
In his address at Hillsborough Castle,
King Charles referred to the
momentous changes in Northern
Ireland that his mother had witnessed
during her reign and he pledged to
follow her 'shining example'.

THE DEVOLVED NATIONS of Scotland, Wales and Northern Ireland play a key part in the unwritten constitution of the United Kingdom. Their importance was acknowledged by The King's visits to all three in the days following his mother's death.

On 13 September, The King and Queen flew from Edinburgh to Belfast for what would be the first visit to Northern Ireland of a male monarch since 1945, though Her late Majesty visited on 22 occasions.

Hundreds of people gathered in Royal Hillsborough, lining the Main Street of the village in the hope of seeing The King and Queen on their brief walkabout. This was followed by a meeting with political leaders at Hillsborough Castle, the official residence of the monarch and of the Secretary of State for Northern Ireland. At a reception at the castle, the speaker of the Northern Ireland Assembly offered a message of condolence on behalf of the people of Northern Ireland. The King responded by speaking of Queen Elizabeth II and the peace process before pledging to 'seek the welfare' of all Northern Ireland's people.

The visit ended with a service of reflection for Her late Majesty's life at St Anne's Cathedral in Belfast, where The King and Queen met leaders from all the major faiths in Northern Ireland.

Lying-in-State, Westminster Hall, 15 September 2022

THE MEDIEVAL RITUAL OF A SOVEREIGN Lying-in-State at Westminster Hall was brought back for King Edward VII. In 1910 his coffin was placed on a catafalque (a raised platform) in the centre of the Hall, and hundreds of thousands of members of the public took the opportunity to file past his coffin and pay their respects. When his son, King George V, died in 1936, another ancient tradition was revived, that of the Vigil of the Princes. His four sons – King Edward VIII, the Duke of York (later King George VI), the Duke of Gloucester and the Duke of Kent – held vigil at the four corners of the catafalque. As a child, Queen Elizabeth II herself was taken to her grandfather's Lying-in-State and was impressed by how still her uncle, the new king, stood: 'he never moved a muscle,' she reported afterwards. 'Not even an eyelid. It was wonderful. And everyone was so quiet. As if the King were asleep.'

When it came to her own Lying-in-State, the silence was equally profound. Set on a raised platform covered in purple velvet, the coffin was draped in the Royal Standard and topped with the Imperial State Crown, the Sovereign's Orb and the Sovereign's Sceptre and a wreath of white roses and dahlias that was renewed every day. Each corner of the platform was guarded around the clock by members of the Household Cavalry, the Foot Guards and The King's Ceremonial Bodyguards, the Gentlemen at Arms, the Royal Company of Archers and the Yeomen of the Guard. Four soldiers from each stood silent vigil for 20 minutes at a time, with two in reserve.

A service attended by The King, members of the Royal Family and members of the House of Lords and the House of Commons was held on Wednesday 14 September before the Lying-in-State began.

As he had done for Her late Majesty's Lying-at-Rest in St Giles' Cathedral in Edinburgh, The King led his brothers and sister in a vigil held on 15 September. Two days later Queen Elizabeth II's eight grandchildren held a similar vigil in the silent hall as members of the public filed past.

King Charles stands respectfully in silent vigil before the coffin of the late Queen Elizabeth II along with his sister and brothers.

Wales welcomes The King and Queen, 16 September 2022

TOP:
'Wales had a special place in my mother's heart', The King said in his first address as Sovereign in the Chamber of the Senedd Cymru (Welsh Parliament).

BOTTOM:
Well-wishers lining the streets of Cardiff to greet The King and Queen.

AFTER A WEEK OF INTENSIVE DUTIES, The King and Queen rested for a day in private, before finishing their tour of the UK's devolved nations with a visit to Wales on 16 September. As the longest-serving Prince of Wales in history – a title that is now held by his eldest son and heir, Prince William – The King has a special relationship with the Welsh nation and has visited on many occasions. Before his investiture as Prince of Wales at Caernarfon Castle in 1969, he took Welsh lessons at Aberystwyth University and as a mark of respect for the culture of Wales, The King spoke in both Welsh and English when he addressed the Senedd Cymru (the Welsh Parliament) in Cardiff.

It was The King's second visit to the Welsh Parliament in less than a year. In October 2021 he had opened the Sixth Senedd (2021–26), accompanying Queen Elizabeth II on her last visit to Wales. This time, The King and Queen arrived by helicopter to be greeted by a gun salute at Cardiff Castle and by the crowds of well-wishers lining the streets of the Welsh capital. Further crowds cheered the royal couple all the way to Llandaff, a mile north of the city centre, home to Cardiff's ancient cathedral. Here they were greeted by a fanfare of trumpeters from the Regimental Band of The Royal Welsh. Hymns were sung in English and Welsh at the Service of Thanksgiving for the Life of Queen Elizabeth II, including the traditional Welsh song, 'Cwm Rhondda' ('Guide Me, O Thou Great Redeemer').

Afterwards, The King and Queen met schoolchildren in the crowd before attending the condolence event at the Senedd in Cardiff Bay and a reception at Cardiff Castle, where The King held an audience with the First Minister of Wales, Mark Drakeford.

'The Queue', London, 14–18 September 2022

TWO DAYS BEFORE WESTMINSTER HALL was due to open to the public, a queue began to form outside the Palace of Westminster, made up of those who wanted to be among the first to express their condolences in person at Her late Majesty's Lying-in-State. Undeterred by the weather and warnings of a long, cold wait, thousands of people stood in line for up to 30 hours to pay their last respects. Symbolising the national mood, the spontaneous gathering of mourners soon became known simply as 'The Queue' as it snaked from Westminster, across the Thames and for six miles along the South Bank to Southwark Park.

The sheer number of people determined to pass by Her late Majesty's coffin meant that the authorities soon made 'The Queue' official. Hundreds of police and volunteer marshals were assigned to assist at checkpoints set up along the route to inspect the special wristbands given to each mourner marking their place in the queue. Amenities such as water fountains, portable toilets and first-aid stations could be found along the route while a live tracker provided information on the length of the queue at any point.

During the afternoon of Saturday 17 September, The King accompanied by The Prince of Wales paid a surprise visit to greet some of those waiting along the South Bank.

The State Funeral, 19 September 2022

T HE DAY OF THE LATE QUEEN'S State Funeral and Committal came at the end of a momentous ten-day period, marked by intensive ceremonial and constitutional formalities and by less formal opportunities to meet fellow mourners and well-wishers across the UK. For the country, it was time to say goodbye to Britain's longest-reigning and much-loved monarch, Queen Elizabeth II.

Westminster Hall closed to the public before dawn. A new wreath was placed on the coffin, this one bearing a single handwritten card: *In loving and devoted memory. Charles R.*

The State Funeral Service in Westminster Abbey was followed by a solemn military procession as Her late Majesty's coffin was borne on the State Gun Carriage from Westminster Abbey to Wellington Arch at Hyde Park Corner, where it was transferred to the State Hearse for the drive to Windsor.

More crowds lined the route to watch the procession along the Long Walk to Windsor Castle, passing Her late Majesty's Fell pony, Emma, and continuing through the Quadrangle where her two corgis, Muick and Sandy, had been brought to watch their royal mistress's final journey.

The Committal service was held in St George's Chapel. During the service, the symbols of Her late Majesty's earthly authority – the Imperial State Crown, the Sovereign's Orb and the Sovereign's Sceptre – were removed from the coffin, where they had been placed for the Lying-in-State, and set on the altar. The Lord Chamberlain, Queen Elizabeth II's most senior official, then broke his wand of office in two and put the halves on the coffin, which was lowered into the Royal Vault to the sound of a lament played by the Sovereign's Piper. The public pomp and ceremony of the funeral ended with the singing of the National Anthem, with words that had last been heard in St George's Chapel more than 70 years previously – 'God Save The King'– marking the final end of one reign and the start of another.

OPPOSITE:
The Lord Chamberlain breaks his wand of office to symbolise that his term of service to Queen Elizabeth II has ended. The wand, a long wooden stick, was once used to admonish courtiers by tapping them if they behaved in a disrespectful manner towards the monarch.

A NEW REIGN

The King

Born Prince Charles Philip Arthur George at Buckingham Palace on 14 November 1948, His Majesty was the first child of the then Princess Elizabeth and the Duke of Edinburgh, and grandson of King George VI. When Queen Elizabeth II ascended the throne as a young mother of 25, Prince Charles became heir apparent and Duke of Cornwall aged just three. Formally presented with the title of Prince of Wales at an investiture ceremony at Caernarfon Castle in 1969, His Majesty was to be the longest-serving Prince of Wales in British history, acceding to the throne on 8 September 2022 at the age of 74.

During his five decades as Prince of Wales, The King was able to champion a wide variety of causes about which he felt deeply. A firm believer in the importance of harmony and sustainability, he was at the forefront of the fight against climate change and biodiversity loss and has spoken passionately about the need to conserve the natural world for future generations. His Majesty has worked for many years to encourage inter-faith dialogue and a greater understanding of different religions. In addition to supporting charities working across all areas of public life, he founded a number of organisations focused particularly on strengthening communities and providing opportunities for disadvantaged young people.

As Sovereign, His Majesty has had to step back from much of the work he did as Prince of Wales. His role now is a unifying one, bringing people together across all sections of society, and as he undertakes State and ceremonial duties, he represents stability and continuity.

His Majesty has two sons: Prince William, born on 21 June 1982, and Prince Harry, born on 15 September 1984. His five grandchildren are Prince George of Wales, Princess Charlotte of Wales, Prince Louis of Wales, Prince Archie of Sussex and Princess Lilibet of Sussex.

The Queen

Her Majesty, as Duchess of Cornwall, visits a reading scheme at St Mary's Primary School, in Battersea, London, January 2013.

THE QUEEN WAS BORN Camilla Rosemary Shand on 17 July 1947 at King's College Hospital in London. On her marriage to the then Prince of Wales in 2005, she took the title Duchess of Cornwall until she became Queen Consort at her husband's Accession as King Charles III.

As well as supporting her husband, His Majesty The King, in his work and role as monarch, Queen Camilla is the Patron or President of more than one hundred organisations and champions a number of causes and issues close to her own heart. Her Majesty is particularly passionate about literacy and empowering women.

As someone who understands not only the joy of reading but also the importance of literacy in creating life opportunities, Her Majesty is an important advocate for written and spoken communication in the UK and internationally. Publishing her own favourite book recommendations during the Coronavirus pandemic lockdown in 2020 met with a hugely positive response and led ultimately to the establishment of her own book club, 'The Queen's Reading Room'. The club, which became a charity in February 2023, aims to help more people find and connect with books that enrich their lives, turning them into lifelong readers.

Her Majesty has also been a great supporter of women's causes and was the first member of the Royal Family to chair meetings and support groups related to sexual assault and domestic abuse. For more than a decade, she has sought to highlight the work of organisations supporting victims of rape and sexual assault, and to break taboos around the subject. She is Patron of the charity SafeLives and has visited Refuge and Women's Aid centres around the UK and overseas to learn more about the issues, meet survivors and highlight the invaluable contribution made by the people and organisations working in this area.

All Change: new cyphers, stamps and currency

THE ROYAL CYPHER IS THE SOVEREIGN'S monogram, a visual representation of the Crown that is used on government buildings, state documents or in any other setting that requires the stamp of royal authority. Designed by the College of Arms, The King's new cypher illustrates both change and continuity. The intertwined initials 'C' for 'Charles' and 'R' for 'Rex' (Latin for 'King') and the royal number 'III' (the roman numeral 3) are topped with the Tudor Crown, traditionally associated with male monarchs and used in the cyphers of Kings Edward VII, George V and George VI. In Scotland, The King's cypher uses the Scottish crown.

A new cypher was also designed for Queen Camilla by Professor Ewan Clayton, combining her initial 'C' for 'Camilla' and 'R' for 'Regina' (Latin for 'Queen'). The monogram will be used by The Queen on personal letterheads, cards and gifts.

The image of the monarch has featured on coins in the UK for more than a thousand years. In a tradition dating back to the 17th century, each monarch faces in the opposite direction to their predecessor – a convention broken only in the brief reign of King Edward VIII who insisted that his profile faced left, as his father's had done, to show the parting in his hair. As Queen Elizabeth II's coinage portrait showed her facing right, King Charles III's faces left. It was designed for the Royal Mint by sculptor Martin Jennings and was personally approved by The King. In a break with tradition, the pared-back design does not feature a crown or any other royal symbols; the Royal Mail explained that the request was for a 'simple' approach, with 'no embellishment'.

The King sat for a separate portrait to be used on banknotes although the new notes will only be released gradually as those featuring the portrait of Queen Elizabeth II are withdrawn from circulation. Stamps featuring Her late Majesty will be phased out in a similar way, to be replaced by those with the new silhouette of King Charles III, a process that collectors know as 'mixed franking' if the stamps of two different monarchs are used on one letter.

The First State Visit, 22 November 2022

STATE VISITS PLAY A KEY ROLE in strengthening Britain's diplomatic and commercial relations with other countries around the world. Invitations to or from Heads of State are issued or accepted on the advice of the Foreign and Commonwealth Office. Incoming Visits, hosted by The King at Buckingham Palace, Windsor Castle or, on occasion, at the Palace of Holyroodhouse, involve impressive displays of pageantry and a State Banquet, and are planned in meticulous detail several months in advance.

For his first incoming State Visit on 22 November 2022, King Charles III and Queen Camilla played host to President Cyril Ramaphosa, the President of the Republic of South Africa. The President was given a ceremonial welcome at Horse Guards Parade before travelling to Buckingham Palace in a carriage procession escorted by mounted soldiers from the Household Cavalry. At the Palace, His Majesty invited President Ramaphosa to view a special display of objects and photographs from the Royal Collection and the Royal Archives with a historic connection to South Africa.

A State Banquet was held in the President's honour that evening, a glittering occasion for which the Ballroom at Buckingham Palace was transformed with a U-shaped table to seat the 150 guests with cultural, diplomatic or commercial links to South Africa. Before dinner was served, The King made a speech emphasising the closeness of the two nations and recalling his mother's visit to Cape Town in 1947. In his reply, President Ramaphosa mentioned Nelson Mandela's visits to the UK and looked forward to a new relationship between the two nations. The end of the banquet was signalled by the arrival of 12 pipers accompanied by The King's Piper, a tradition that dates back to Queen Victoria.

The King's speech at the State Banquet held in honour of South African President Cyril Ramaphosa referred back to his mother's visit in 1947; it was in Cape Town that she celebrated her 21st birthday, later making her famous speech pledging her life to the devoted service of the Commonwealth.

The First Christmas Broadcast, 25 December 2022

In his Christmas Broadcast (opposite), The King remembered his visit to Bethlehem and the Church of the Nativity in 2020 (above), speaking of Christmas as a celebration across the boundaries of faith and belief, united by 'the power of light overcoming darkness'.

KING GEORGE V DELIVERED the first ever Christmas Broadcast in 1932, making good use of 'one of the marvels of modern science' as he put it in his speech. He was referring to the BBC's Empire Service, the English-language broadcasts that were established to connect English-speakers in the far reaches of what was then the British Empire. That address was heard by an estimated 22 million people in Australia, Canada, India, Kenya, South Africa and the UK. So popular was it that the king made his Christmas message an annual event, a tradition followed by King George VI and Queen Elizabeth II.

For Her late Majesty, the Christmas broadcast provided a rare opportunity to express her own feelings about the year's events and developments and to connect some of her personal experiences to those of her audience. For that reason, 3pm on Christmas Day has become an essential part of the Christmas festivities for many families, proving a moment of reflection that has reinforced the monarch's role as a focus of national unity.

That sense of continuity was reinforced by King Charles III in his first Christmas Broadcast on 25 December 2022. At the end of a momentous year, he paid tribute to his mother and reflected on a period of anxiety and hardship, both at home and abroad. More than 10.7 million viewers watched his televised message, shown simultaneously on several television channels in the UK, making it the most popular Christmas Day broadcast by a monarch since official viewing figures began.

Greeting Ambassadors

ONE OF THE KEY ELEMENTS of The King's role is to support the UK's diplomatic relations with other nations. On a day-to-day level this means granting an audience to newly arrived Ambassadors and High Commissioners, the most senior diplomats representing their countries. At any given time there are more than 170 Ambassadors and High Commissioners (the latter representing Commonwealth nations) in the UK, and each will have an Audience with The King shortly after taking up their role.

There has been little change in the format of diplomatic audiences since the 19th century. The diplomat and his or her spouse are collected from their residence or embassy by one of the Royal Mews's horse-drawn carriages, known as a State Landau. They are driven to Buckingham Palace, accompanied by the Marshal of the Diplomatic Corps, who travels in a second carriage.

The Audience begins with the diplomat presenting his or her Letters of Commission (for High Commissioners) or Letters of Credence (for Ambassadors). These formal letters, also known as Credentials, are from the diplomat's Head of State to The King, asking him to give 'credence' to the new Ambassador or High Commissioner and assuring him that the new appointee can speak on behalf of his or her country.

For the rest of the audience, The King and the visiting diplomat speak informally, often about current issues in the Ambassador or High Commissioner's home country. Conversations are entirely private and no written transcript or recording is ever made. This is also true of political and other Audiences which occur regularly throughout His Majesty's working week.

The first Credentials of King Charles III's reign were presented by the Ambassador of Ukraine, Vadym Prystaiko, and the High Commissioner of Pakistan, Moazzam Ahmad Khan, at Buckingham Palace in October 2022.

On 27 October 2022, The King held an audience with His Excellency Nehemia Sekhonyana Bereng, High Commissioner for the Kingdom of Lesotho, and his wife, Ntee Constance Bereng.

Maundy Money

The first Royal Maundy service in the reign of His Majesty King Charles III took place at York Minster on 6 April 2023, when 74 men and 74 women chosen from Anglican and Ecumenical communities across the UK received a gift from The King to thank them for their outstanding Christian service.

T HE FIRST RECORDS OF AN ENGLISH MONARCH distributing money and clothing to the poor to mark Maundy Thursday (named after Christ's command, or 'mandate', to his Disciples to 'love one another') dates from the reign of King John when, in 1210, the royal household's accounts record his gifts of 13 silver coins to 13 poor men – symbolically representing Christ and his 12 Apostles.

Maundy Thursday occurs in Holy Week, the day that Jesus washed the feet of his Disciples as an act of humility and shared a Last Supper with them before his trial and Crucifixion the following day. Charles II established the practice of sending an official to distribute the Maundy Money, but King George V reinstated the royal custom of distributing the gifts in person in 1932.

The number of coins distributed each year now reflects the number of years the monarch has lived. Thus at the ceremony that took place at York Minster on 6 April 2023, the 74-year-old King Charles III presented specially minted Maundy Money, bearing the coinage portrait of the monarch (see page 36), to 74 male and 74 female pensioners in a white leather purse. The coins have a face value of 74 pence, and are legal tender, though their symbolic value is such that recipients prefer to keep them. Instead, The King gives them a second red purse containing a small amount of ordinary coinage in lieu of gifts of food and clothing.

Birthday Cards and Wedding Anniversaries

I N A TRADITION DATING BACK TO 1917, when King George V sent a telegram of good wishes to anyone celebrating a 100th birthday or a 60th wedding anniversary, the first birthday cards with a congratulatory message signed by The King and Queen were delivered in October 2022. No cards were issued during the period of mourning for Queen Elizabeth II, and a new card featuring a photograph of the royal couple taken in the summer of 2018 had to be designed and printed before the first congratulatory cards of the new reign could be posted.

Over the century, the number of cards signed by the monarch has grown significantly thanks to the substantial growth in the UK population during the reign of the late Queen, combined with improvements in health care. King George V sent 24 telegrams to centenarians in 1917, while 273 were delivered in 1952, the year of Queen Elizabeth II's Accession. Today, the number of people in the UK living to the age of 100 has risen to 15,834 (as of 2020), and everyone receives a card. A second card is sent to anyone celebrating their 105th birthday, and another card every year after that.

The King and Queen have also continued the tradition of sending a card to couples celebrating their 60th, 65th and 70th wedding anniversaries.

Ruth Park-Pearson (right) who celebrated her 100th birthday on 21 October 2022 was one of the first recipients of the new birthday card. Mrs Park-Pearson served in the Women's Royal Naval Service (Wrens) during the Second World War.

PLANNING
THE CORONATION

'Operation Golden Orb'

PREVIOUS PAGE:
Abbey staff installing new candles in the chandeliers above the Coronation Chair. Behind them on the High Altar are the candelabra and communion plate made for use in the royal chapels in the late 17th century. Together with the other items of regalia, the plate is normally on display with the rest of the Crown Jewels in the Tower of London.

OPPOSITE, TOP:
The official invitation for the Coronation was designed by heraldic artist Andrew Jamieson. Encompassing Their Majesties' coats of arms, the design also features the Green Man, a figure from British folklore, symbolic of spring and rebirth, the floral emblems of the four nations of the UK and flora and fauna of a typical wildflower meadow, representing The King's love of the natural world.

OPPOSITE, BOTTOM:
Flowers for the Coronation were chosen to reflect the best of the season's blossoms from sources in the UK and are shown here in the Abbey Chapter House being arranged by floral designer Shane Connolly.

CORONATION IS AN EXTRAORDINARILY complex occasion: it is a royal spectacle, a religious service and a major State occasion requiring a mastery of logistics, ceremonial and liturgy. Code named 'Operation Golden Orb', preparations for King Charles III's Coronation began well before the date of 6 May 2023 was announced in October 2022. Committees were set up to co-ordinate the activities of the Royal Household, Church, Government, armed forces, security services, the media and other stakeholders, led, as is customary, by the Duke of Norfolk in his hereditary role as Earl Marshal.

These committees were charged not only with organising and running the Coronation Service at Westminster Abbey but also with all the other elements of a major State event. They had to consider myriad details, from the altering of crowns to crowd management and street cleaning; from the design of invitations and the logistics of accommodating foreign royalty and Heads of State, to the thousands of additional troops and police required for the processions and for security.

Although the order of service dates back many centuries, all coronations are distinct in their own way. Over time, the service has been changed and adapted to suit the circumstances of the age and the personal preferences of the monarch. The organisation of the Coronation of King Charles III was influenced in part by the 1937 coronation of King George VI and Queen Elizabeth, the last in which a Queen Consort was crowned, but also reflected The King's personal commitment to diversity and sustainability. The service was rooted in the longstanding traditions and pageantry of the monarchy and much of the planning involved the modification of historic objects and robes while ensuring that any changes made to the regalia were completely reversible.

Of the 2,300 people attending the Coronation ceremony, 850 people were invited in recognition of their charitable contributions, including 450 recipients of a British Empire Medal. In addition, 400 young people from groups chosen by the Royal Family and the Government watched the Coronation from St Margaret's Church, which stands alongside the Abbey.

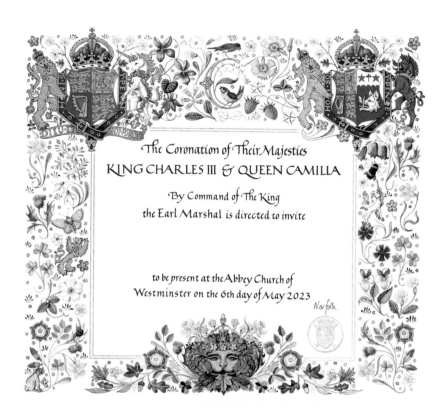

The Coronation of Their Majesties

KING CHARLES III & QUEEN CAMILLA

By Command of The King
the Earl Marshal is directed to invite

to be present at the Abbey Church of
Westminster on the 6th day of May 2023

Norfolk.

Setting the Scene: Westminster Abbey

TOP LEFT:
The service to celebrate the arrival of the Stone of Destiny at Westminster Abbey was held on 29 April 2023 just inside the west door of the Abbey close to the poppy-lined Tomb of the Unknown Warrior.

TOP RIGHT:
A rehearsal space was constructed in the Ballroom at Buckingham Palace, carefully mapped out to match the dimensions of the Coronation Theatre within the Abbey. Various chairs used during the Coronation Service were used for rehearsals, except for the Coronation Chair itself – a smaller chair of a similar design was borrowed from the Abbey, and a cushion was added to achieve the correct height of the real seat.

BOTTOM:
The Coronation Chair underwent conservation before the Coronation. Its surface was gently cleaned and the surviving layers of gilding carefully stabilised. The graffiti visible on the back of the chair was made by schoolboys and visitors in the 18th and 19th centuries.

WESTMINSTER ABBEY HAS BEEN THE SITE of the coronation of every British monarch since William the Conqueror, with only two exceptions, and King Charles III was the 40th reigning monarch to be crowned there. In 1953, the Abbey had to be closed for five months to allow for the building of stands to seat 8,000 people and an annexe containing special robing rooms, but for King Charles III's Coronation, with its focus on sustainability – and on health and safety grounds – the guest list was limited to the 2,300 seats already available in the Abbey.

The Order of Service includes rites dating back to the 10th century that require the creation of a ceremonial space known as the Coronation Theatre. It is here, close to the High Altar, that the Coronation Chair was placed and where The King sat for the Crowning and Investiture components of the Coronation Service. A replica of the theatre was built at Buckingham Palace to be used for rehearsals in the run up to the Coronation, although dress rehearsals took place in the Abbey itself.

As part of the preparations for the Coronation, the Coronation Chair, normally displayed in St George's Chapel at the west end of the Abbey, had to be cleaned and conserved. This remarkable piece of furniture was made for Edward I in 1301 and has been the central focus of coronations ever since. The oak chair has long lost its painted and carved decoration, but the base survives. This was built to enclose the symbolic Stone of Scone (also known as the Stone of Destiny), a block of red sandstone from Scone Abbey, Perthshire, used as the coronation seat by Scottish kings. Seized from the Scots by the forces of Edward I in 1296, it was returned to Edinburgh in 1996 and now only leaves Scotland for a coronation in Westminster Abbey. Prior to the Coronation, the Stone was blessed in a special service in Edinburgh and again on its safe arrival at Westminster Abbey. The massive stone has two iron rings attached, through which a carrying bar is inserted. Iron bars located underneath the throne support the Stone, which weighs just over 152 kg (336lb).

Music for the Coronation

OPPOSITE:
Westminster Abbey Sub-Organist Peter Holder practising for the Coronation at the console of the mighty Harrison & Harrison instrument, installed for the coronation of King George VI in 1937.

BELOW:
A moment of infectious joy was created by the Ascension Choir who sang a specially composed piece by Debbie Wiseman called 'Alleluia (O Sing Praises)', using words from the first two verses of Psalm 47. The piece was performed by eight singers drawn from the Kingdom Choir, a Gospel group based in the south east of England.

A LIFE-LONG MUSIC ENTHUSIAST and champion of the arts, His Majesty was personally involved in planning and commissioning the Coronation music programme, which brought together esteemed composers and performers in a blend of classical and church traditions and new musical voices from the worlds of contemporary film, television and musical theatre.

Twelve new compositions were commissioned for the Coronation, five of which were performed before the service began, prior to the arrival of Their Majesties at the Abbey. They included a piece called 'Be Thou my Vision' based on His Majesty's favourite hymn, jointly composed by Nigel Hess, Roderick Williams and Shirley Thompson. This was performed by the Coronation Orchestra, made up of members of the eight leading orchestras of which the former Prince of Wales was Patron, conducted by Sir Antonio Pappano, Music Director of the Royal Opera House. Also performing in the pre-service music was Alis Huws, the Royal Harpist, who performed a setting of a Welsh folk song, 'Tros y Garreg' ('Crossing the Stone') by Sir Karl Jenkins. The Monteverdi Choir and Orchestra and English Baroque Soloists opened the celebrations with music by J.S. Bach and Bruckner under the baton of Sir John Eliot Gardiner.

Choristers from five choirs, including those of Westminster Abbey and His Majesty's Chapel Royal, St James's Palace, joined forces under Andrew Nethsingha, the Abbey's Organist and Master of the Choristers, for the main service, which was notable for Paul Mealor's 'Coronation Kyrie', sung in Welsh by Sir Bryn Terfel, and Roxanna Panufnik's flamboyant 'Coronation Sanctus'. Raising the roof with Debbie Wiseman's 'O Sing Praises' was the Ascension Choir, the first Gospel choir to sing at a coronation, and further exuberance was provided by the Lord Lloyd-Webber's anthem, 'Make A Joyful Noise', based on Psalm 98, which began and ended with fanfares from the trumpeters of the Royal Air Force.

The Robes of His Majesty The King

THE CORONATION SERVICE INVOLVES several changes of robe for the Sovereign, each with its own significance, and in the interests of sustainability, The King reused several robes from the Royal Collection.

The King entered the Abbey wearing the crimson Robe of State (also known as the Parliamentary Robe because it is worn by the monarch at the State Opening of Parliament). This was worn at the coronations of King George V in 1911 and King George VI in 1937. Due to its fragile state, the velvet upper was carefully conserved by the Royal School of Needlework and the Robe was finished and fitted by the royal robemakers Ede & Ravenscroft.

Along with the other symbols of kingship, the Robe was removed before the Anointing, for which The King wore a cream silk shirt with his naval uniform trousers, indicating that he was 'uncovered' and in a state of humility before God. For the Investiture, he was first dressed in another simple white garment known as the Colobium Sindonis (Latin for 'tunic of the shroud'), which was originally worn by The King's grandfather, King George VI, for his coronation in 1937.

Over the Colobium Sindonis he wore the cloth-of-gold Supertunica, embroidered with national symbols and lined with crimson silk. Made for the coronation of King George V in 1911, the Supertunica has been worn at every coronation since. Over the Supertunica, The King wore the Imperial Mantle originally made for George IV in 1821, making it the oldest of the vestments used in the Coronation Service. By contrast, the Stole Royal was the only new vestment made for The King especially for the Coronation. It was worn with the Girdle, also known as the Coronation Sword Belt, used by King George VI at his coronation in 1937. Lastly, The King wore the gold embroidered Coronation Glove on his right hand, also made for King George VI in 1937.

At the end of the ceremony, after the Coronation and Homage, The King withdrew to St Edward's Chapel and exchanged the Investiture robes for a purple Coronation Tunic and the purple Robe of Estate in which he left the Abbey. Not to be confused with the Robe of State, the Robe of Estate worn by The King was originally made for King George V and was worn by King George VI. It was this Robe in which King Charles III subsequently posed for his official Coronation portraits.

The Robes of Her Majesty The Queen

OPPOSITE:
For her official Coronation portrait, The Queen wore the gown designed for her by the celebrated couturier Bruce Oldfield, with its intricate gold embroidery personalised with the names of her children and grandchildren.

RIGHT:
Embroiderers from the Royal School of Needlework at work on Her Majesty's new Robe of Estate.

BELOW:
This detail from The Queen's Coronation gown shows the cuffs used to embellish each sleeve embroidered in gold with the floral emblems of the four nations of the UK on a background of intertwined daisies, forget-me-nots, celandines and scarlet pimpernels.

QUEEN CAMILLA ENTERED THE ABBEY wearing the Robe of State made for the coronation of Queen Elizabeth II and used at subsequent State Openings of Parliament. The gown worn under the Robe had been kept a carefully guarded secret until the moment The Queen entered Westminster Abbey. Designed by Bruce Oldfield and created in his couture workrooms in London, the impeccably crafted dress was constructed from soft satin-like Peau de Soie (literally 'skin of silk'), made in Suffolk, and had bracelet-length sleeves and a wide neckline to display the Coronation necklace. This spectacular necklace was made by Garrard for Queen Victoria in 1858 and has been worn by successive Queen Consorts (Queen Alexandra, Queen Mary and Queen Elizabeth The Queen Mother) and by the late Queen Elizabeth II at their coronations. Embroidered flower garlands decorated the gown's short train, and a cut-away front revealed an embroidered underskirt featuring Her Majesty's cypher flanked by Bluebell and Beth, The Queen's Jack Russell terriers, who were adopted from Battersea Dogs and Cats Home in 2017. The underskirt also included the embroidered names of The Queen's children (Tom and Laura) and five grandchildren (Lola, Freddy, Eliza, Louis and Gus). The Queen's matching shoes, made from the same material as the dress, were designed by Elliot Zed.

The Coaches and Horses of the Royal Mews

OPPOSITE, TOP:
Queen Elizabeth II's cypher having been carefully removed, The King's cypher is attached to the arm of a postilion's uniform, ready to be worn on Coronation Day.

OPPOSITE, BOTTOM:
A conservator removes the backs of one of the horsehair cushions from the interior of the Gold State Coach.

BELOW:
The cypher of King Charles III set within the motto of the Order of the Garter, the order of chivalry founded by Edward III in 1348: 'Honi soit que mal y pense' ('Shame on him who thinks evil of it').

THE ROYAL MEWS AT BUCKINGHAM PALACE is home to the horse-drawn coaches and carriages that are key to the pomp and pageantry for which the British monarchy is famous. It was here that the 9m (29-foot) long Gold State Coach was refurbished ahead of its starring role in the post-Coronation procession, from Westminster Abbey to Buckingham Palace (see page 104). Eight Windsor Greys, originally bred in Ireland, are used to pull the massive coach. The Greys are trained by drawing a carriage laden with rubber tyres to which sandbags are progressively added until it reaches four tons, being the weight of the Gold State Coach. Meanwhile, the State Harness was repaired and cleaned, its gilt metal polished to a high shine, and, fashioned from recycled plastic, new royal blue rosettes and mane dressings were ordered to decorate the harness for the procession.

More than 160 new cyphers were made to adorn the Royal Mews livery in time for the Coronation. Each cypher was hand-embroidered and carefully attached to the uniforms of the postilions who ride and handle the horses, and the grooms and footmen who walk alongside the horses in royal processions. The new cyphers replaced those of Queen Elizabeth II, some of which dated back to the coronation in 1953.

The Gold State Coach is the oldest and most spectacular coach in the collection at the Royal Mews and has been used at every coronation since that of William IV in 1831. Designed for the coronation of George III in 1761, although not completed in time (to his regret), the coach cost £8,000 to build (the equivalent of more than £1.5m today). The age and fragility of the coach means that it is only used for the most special of occasions. The conservation process took several months and included careful assessments of the spectacular giltwood elements and the painted surfaces of the exterior, as well as treatment of the interior upholstery. The holders for the Sovereign's Sceptre and Orb were refurbished, the interior side panels were restored and new seat cushions were made, stuffed with horsehair in the traditional manner.

Many skilled hands were involved in preparing clothing and regalia for the Coronation using traditional techniques dating back to the Middle Ages. This was an opportunity to revive and reuse objects of great historical and cultural significance, and to commission new works that will now themselves become important souvenirs of a momentous occasion.

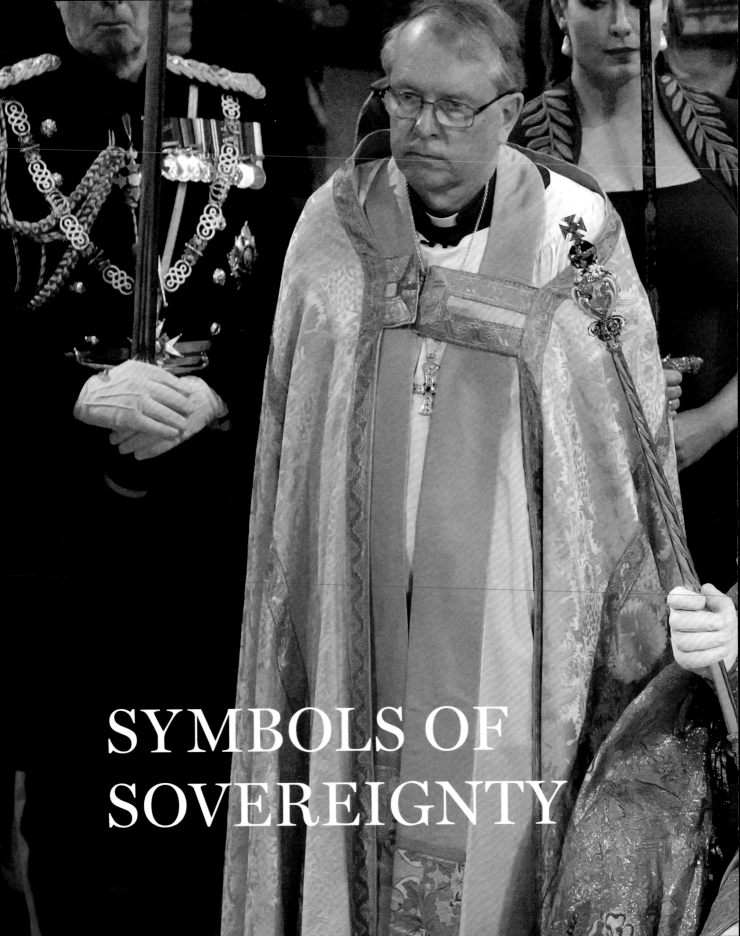

SYMBOLS OF
SOVEREIGNTY

Royal Regalia Remade

OPPOSITE:
The Jewelled Sword of Offering
(see page 70) being cleaned by
The King's Armourer in preparation
for its use in the Coronation ceremony
to symbolise the knightly virtues of
the protection of good and the
punishment of evil.

BELOW:
St Edward's Crown being taken apart
and adjusted to sit comfortably on the
head of The King by Mark Appleby (of
Mappin & Webb), the Crown Jeweller.
The post of Crown Jeweller was
created in 1843 by Queen Victoria and
includes responsibility for maintaining
all the ceremonial objects making up
the Crown Jewels of the UK.

THE REGALIA USED IN THE CORONATION of King Charles III carries great symbolic weight, referring to the monarch's role as the ruler of the nation and as Head of the Church of England.

So potent a symbol of sovereignty is the Crown Regalia that when Charles I was executed in 1649 and the monarchy replaced by a Commonwealth, the Parliamentary authorities ordered that the most sacred coronation items were to be 'totallie Broken and defaced' rather than sold. The jewels were prised out of their settings and the denuded frames sent to the Mint to be melted down.

At the Restoration in 1660, Charles II was determined to bring back the magnificence of the monarchy and he ordered a new set of regalia for his coronation in 1661, intended to replicate the originals as closely as possible. The task of re-creating the regalia was entrusted to Sir Robert Vyner (1631–88), who was appointed Royal Goldsmith in 1660. Today the artefacts he created remain the central components of the Coronation and of the Crown Jewels, which are usually on display in the Tower of London.

Just as important for symbolising The King's role as the Head of the Church in England is the chalice and paten used for distributing the bread and wine of Communion at the Coronation. Made of gold, they form part of a set of altar plate also commissioned by Charles II from Robert Vyner, who appears to have collaborated with his uncle, Thomas Vyner, whose hallmark is stamped on the patten and chalice. Robert Vyner outsourced the work to a number of other goldsmiths and he acted as banker to the king, funding the cost of the new regalia from his own pocket to the tune of £12,184 (equivalent to £30m at today's prices), later reclaiming the cost from the Crown.

Every item of regalia had to be carefully cleaned and prepared for the Coronation, while the crowns – St Edward's Crown, the lighter Imperial State Crown worn by The King, and Queen Mary's Crown, worn by The Queen – were adjusted to fit comfortably by the Crown Jeweller at Mappin & Webb.

Spoon, Spurs and Sword

THE CORONATION SPOON is the oldest item in the regalia and the only piece to survive the Commonwealth. First recorded in 1349 as part of St Edward's regalia, it was already being described as a spoon of 'antique forme' and it is thought to date from the 12th century, having been made for Henry II or Richard I. The Spoon was among the royal jewels that were sold in 1649 by Cromwell's Commissioners. It was bought by a Royalist – a Mr Kynnersley, Yeoman of Charles I's Wardrobe – who returned it to Charles II in 1661, when the four small pearls were added to the decoration.

The Coronation Spoon is used for the most sacred part of the ceremony, when the Archbishop of Canterbury pours holy oil into the bowl of the spoon and anoints the sovereign on his hands, breast and head, in the same way that the Biblical Zadok the Priest anointed Solomon as king of Israel (1 Kings I: 32–39). The holy oil is poured from a gold Ampulla cast in the form of an eagle with outspread wings, with an opening in the beak. The design reflects the 14th-century legend that the Virgin Mary presented a golden eagle and a vial of oil to St Thomas à Becket in a vision, instructing him to use it for anointing future monarchs.

After the anointing, King Charles III put on his historic vestments and was presented with the Spurs. Symbolic of knighthood, they refer to the chivalric ideal of monarchy. Their use in the ceremony dates back to the coronation of Richard I in 1189, when the rituals of knighthood were familiar and full of meaning. Made of gold in a deliberately antiquated design with tiny heel spikes, they imitate a medieval knight's spurs and end in a Tudor rose. In 1820, the spurs were altered for George IV, the original leather buckles and straps being replaced by crimson velvet embroidered with gold thread.

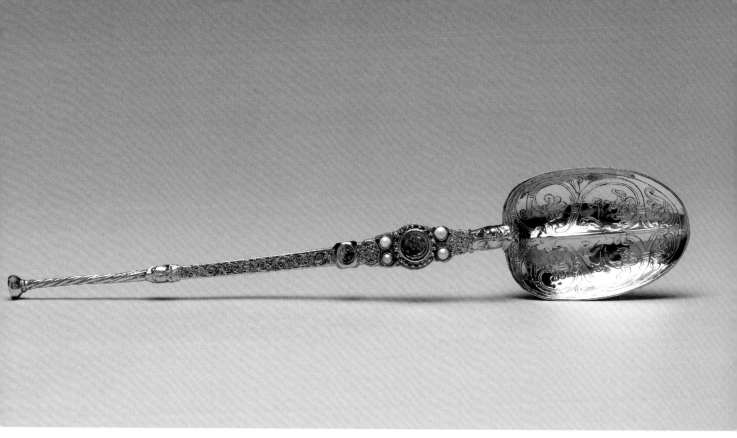

The Jewelled Sword of Offering also represents knightly ideals. Having been blessed by the Archbishop, it is presented to the monarch with the instruction that it should only be used for the protection of good and the punishment of evil.

Whereas most of the regalia was made for Charles II, the Sword of Offering was commissioned by George IV for his coronation in 1821 at a cost of £5,988. An avid art collector, the king was known for his love of extravagance and opulence, and the sword, intended to be part of his private collection, was made to his design. The hilt is covered with diamonds and emeralds while the gold scabbard is set with sapphires, rubies, emeralds and some 2,000 diamonds in the shape of roses, thistles and shamrocks, the national emblems of England, Scotland and Ireland.

Representing dignity, the Coronation Ring is sometimes known as 'the wedding ring of England', after Elizabeth I's reply when asked why she would not take a husband: pointing to the coronation ring on her finger, the queen declared that she was 'already bound unto a husband, which is the kingdom of England'. For many centuries a new coronation ring was made for each monarch and kept as a personal possession but that practice ended in the 20th century, when King Edward VII chose to use William IV's ring, made in 1831, and subsequent sovereigns have followed his example.

After the ring, The King was presented with two hinged bracelets with the words: 'Receive the Bracelets of sincerity and wisdom, both for tokens of the Lord's protection embracing you on every side; and also for symbols and pledges of that bond which unites you with your Peoples.' Also known as Armills, the original bracelets were lost or destroyed during the period of the Commonwealth and velvet-lined bracelets decorated with enamel were made for the coronation of Charles II. These were used at every Coronation from 1661 until 1953, when new versions were made especially for Queen Elizabeth II as a gift from the Governments of the Commonwealth, which then consisted of Australia, Canada, Ceylon (now Sri Lanka), New Zealand, Pakistan, South Africa, Southern Rhodesia (now Zimbabwe) and the United Kingdom. For his Coronation, King Charles chose to use the 17th-century bracelets.

OPPOSITE:
The Jewelled Sword of Offering and the Armills.

BELOW:
The King's Coronation Ring.

RIGHT:
King Charles holds the Jewelled Sword of Offering. This ceremonial sword weighs 3.6 kg (8lb) and was carried prior to its presentation to The King by MP Penny Mordaunt in her role as Lord President of the Privy Council.

The Sovereign's Orb and Sceptres

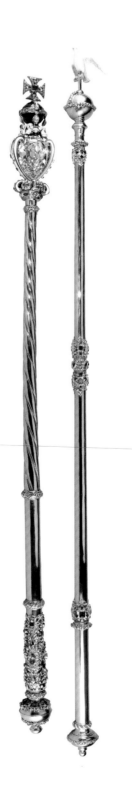

AT A CENTRAL MOMENT in the Coronation ceremony, The King is invested with the symbols of his office: the Orb and Sceptres (the composer William Walton composed a much-loved march for Queen Elizabeth II's coronation which he named 'Orb and Sceptre', but there are, in fact, two sceptres, not one). The Orb, made for Charles II's coronation in 1661, is a hollow gold sphere, representing the earth, encrusted with emeralds, rubies, sapphires, diamonds and pearls. The pearls line the jewelled bands that divide the globe into three segments, representing the three continents known to medieval rulers (Europe, Asia and Africa: the Americas were known by 1661 but the orb was intended to be a replica of Edward the Confessor's 11th-century regalia). The cross that surmounts the Orb represents God's dominion over the world and is a reminder that the monarch has historically been seen as God's earthly representative.

The Sovereign's Sceptre with Dove is made of gold, encircled by jewelled collars and topped with an enamelled dove representing the Holy Ghost. Sometimes called 'The Rod of Equity and Mercy', the Sceptre is handed to the new sovereign as a reminder of their duty of pastoral care.

Its partner, the Sovereign's Sceptre with Cross, represents the sovereign's power and governance on earth, and was the most expensive item of the regalia made for Charles II in 1661, apart from the crowns. The enamelled band, encrusted with diamonds, rubies, sapphires and emeralds, was originally set in the middle of the shaft but was moved to the bottom in 1838 to make it easier for Queen Victoria to hold. Both sceptres are held at the moment of Coronation, the Sceptre with Cross in the right hand and the Sceptre with Dove in the left, while the Orb is placed nearby on the High Altar.

PREVIOUS PAGE:
The Sovereign's Sceptre with
Cross (left) and the Sovereign's
Sceptre with Dove (right),
and the Sovereign's Orb.

OPPOSITE:
Details of the Sceptre heads.

ABOVE:
A detail of the diamond- and pearl-
encrusted cross with an emerald
at its centre from the top of the
Sovereign's Orb, which The King is
holding in his right hand below.

The Sceptre with Cross was transformed in 1911 by the insertion of Cullinan I, the largest of the stones cut from the Cullinan Diamond. Discovered on 26 January 1905 in Pretoria, South Africa, the diamond was named after Thomas Cullinan, the mine's owner. Purchased by the Transvaal government, it was presented as a gift to King Edward VII as a symbol of the healing relationship between Britain and South Africa following the Anglo-Boer Wars (1899–1902). For security, a decoy diamond, guarded by detectives, was sent to London by ship while the real stone was sent by parcel post, both arriving safely. The king named it the 'Great Star of Africa' and when he died in 1910, the Sceptre with Cross was altered to set the great diamond at its top. The Cullinan Diamond still holds the record for being the largest uncut diamond ever found, and Cullinan I, weighing 530 carats, remains the world's largest flawless diamond.

The Imperial State Crown, the Orb and the Sceptre are the three great symbols of royal authority, placed on the coffin of Queen Elizabeth II during her Lying-in-State and funeral, and symbolically removed and set on the altar during the Committal service in St George's Chapel (see page 28), not to be used again until her successor's coronation.

St Edward's Crown

ST EDWARD'S CROWN IS USED only for the moment of Coronation itself and is the most important and sacred item of the ceremony. The original crown was made for Edward the Confessor, the last pre-Norman king of England and founder of Westminster Abbey. When he was canonised in 1161, his crown became a holy relic and the Abbey monks claimed that St Edward had asked them in a vision to ensure that the crown and other regalia were used at all future coronations. Almost every monarch between 1220 and 1626 has followed this injunction.

Since the original was melted down in 1649, Charles II had to commission a replica for his coronation. Made by the Royal Goldsmith Robert Vyner in 1661, this version of St Edward's Crown is set with spectacular jewels. The frame of the crown is made up of crosses, fleurs-de-lis and arches, and the stones are set on white enamel mounts formed by acanthus leaves. The effect must have been dazzling, but the cost was so prohibitive that the jewels were hired and returned after the coronation ceremony. It was not until 1911 that King George V had 444 precious and semi-precious stones set permanently in the crown.

The crown weighs an impressive 2.07 kg (just over 4.5lb) and to mark her Diamond Jubilee in 2012, Queen Elizabeth II was filmed examining the crown and remembering the weight of it on her head. 'Is it still as heavy?', she asked, only to answer her own question by lifting it. 'Yes, it is. It weighs a ton.' Because it is so heavy, some monarchs have chosen lighter crowns for their coronations, with St Edward's Crown resting nearby on the Abbey's High Altar. St Edward's Crown is familiar to many because it is widely used as an emblem for the monarch on a range of artefacts, such as police, ambulance and armed service uniforms; it also formed part of Queen Elizabeth II's royal cypher on letter boxes, telephone kiosks and the royal coat of arms.

The name 'St Edward's Crown' was first used by Henry III (1207–72) who had a special devotion to St Edward the Confessor and who rebuilt the east end of Westminster Abbey as a shrine to the saint. Henry III also commissioned Italian craftsmen to create the magnificent mosaic pavement on which the Coronation of King Charles III took place.

The Imperial State Crown

OPPOSITE:
The Imperial State Crown is worn on many more occasions than St Edward's Crown and has been refashioned many times to fit comfortably on the heads of successive monarchs.

BELOW:
In keeping with tradition, this plaque hidden within the frame of the Imperial State Crown records the adjustments made for the 2023 Coronation.

UNTIL ITS DESTRUCTION during the Civil War, St Edward's Crown was regarded as a relic of Edward the Confessor and was kept permanently at Westminster Abbey. In honour of that tradition, the monarch takes off St Edward's Crown and puts on the Imperial State Crown to leave the Abbey. Made for the coronation of King George VI in 1937 and replicating earlier designs, the Imperial State Crown is a 'working crown', used for every State Opening of Parliament and other royal occasions to symbolise the Sovereign's power and position. It is named not for the British Empire as is sometimes thought, but because the arches that rise from the circular frame meet to form a cross. This style of crown was traditionally associated with the crowns of emperors rather than of kings, and was adopted by the English monarchy following Henry VIII's break with the Roman Catholic Church in the 16th century as a representation of the monarch's earthly power.

Made of gold and set with 2,868 diamonds, 17 sapphires, 11 emeralds, 269 pearls and four rubies, it contains some of the world's most famous jewels. The legends associated with these historic gems are open to challenge but they undoubtedly add to the allure of this spectacular crown.

One such jewel is the Stuart Sapphire, said to have been taken to France by James II when he fled during the Glorious Revolution of 1688. Originally at the front of the Imperial State Crown, it was moved to the back in 1909 to make way for the diamond known as Cullinan II, cut from the largest diamond ever found (see page 74).

The large red gemstone (known as a spinel) at the front of the crown is the legendary Black Prince's Ruby, said to have been part of the English royal collection since the 1360s and, it is claimed, worn by Henry V at the Battle of Agincourt in 1415. A similarly unsubstantiated story surrounds St Edward's Sapphire, set at the centre of the diamond cross that tops the crown. The stone was allegedly taken from the saint's ring in 1163 when his body was reinterred at Westminster Abbey. While the legend reinforces the importance of the English monarchy's links to its ancient and holy predecessor, the sapphire itself was not added to the crown until the Victorian era and is unlikely to have been part of the original ring.

The Queen's Regalia

HER MAJESTY THE QUEEN had her own set of ceremonial regalia for the Coronation, consisting of crown, ring, sceptre and rod. In the interests of sustainability, The Queen chose an existing crown for her regalia rather than commissioning a new one. As a tribute to Queen Elizabeth II, who was especially fond of diamond jewellery, Queen Camilla chose the crown designed for the 1911 coronation of Queen Mary alongside her husband King George V. Queen Mary's crown has 2,200 diamonds in all, and the *Daily Telegraph* reported in 1911 that 'it has no jewels but diamonds, and the diamonds cluster together as if they had no support but their own light'.

This was the first time that an existing crown had been used for a consort's coronation in recent history and various modifications were carried out to suit The Queen's preferences. Four of the eight detachable arches were removed, leaving four elegant arches to support the pear-shaped diamond known as Cullinan III, one of nine large diamonds cut from the Cullinan Diamond in 1907 (see page 74). This diamond, along with Cullinan IV, set in the crown's band, and V, set in the cross above, can all be detached for use in alternative settings. The diamonds formed part of Queen Elizabeth's personal jewellery collection for many years and were often worn by Her late Majesty as brooches.

Mirroring The King's Sceptre with Dove (see page 72), The Queen was invested with the Rod with Dove, symbolising the Holy Ghost and the virtues of equity and mercy. The Queen's Sceptre with Cross, inlaid with rock crystals, was made for Mary Modena, Queen Consort of James II, by the Royal Goldsmith, Robert Vyner, in 1685.

Like The King, The Queen was also presented with a Coronation Ring made in 1831 – for the coronation of Queen Adelaide, Queen Consort to William IV. When it was made, the Lord Chamberlain's office, who paid for the ring, balked at the original estimate of £150 (the equivalent of nearly £14,500 today), but eventually agreed to pay £126 (the equivalent of just over £12,000 today) for 'A Ruby and Brilliant Ring for the Queen'. The ring has been used by three further Queen Consorts: Queen Alexandra (1902), Queen Mary (1911) and Queen Elizabeth (1937).

CORONATION DAY

Countdown to the Coronation

AFTER MONTHS OF PREPARATION, the planning work undertaken by the 'Operation Golden Orb' team was ready to go live. In the week leading up to the Coronation rehearsals took place at Westminster Abbey and along the processional route. In the middle of the night, on 3 May, The Mall was filled with the sound of marching boots and horses' hooves as thousands of soldiers – some mounted on horseback and some on foot – staged a full dress rehearsal of Their Majesties' journeys to and from the Abbey. Eager crowds gathered to watch, some having already camped out along The Mall for more than a week. Later that day, The King and Queen, accompanied by The Prince and Princess of Wales and their three children, attended a Coronation rehearsal in Westminster Abbey, where they were greeted by the Dean of Westminster.

Meanwhile Londoners got used to seeing police outriders on motorbikes escorting heads of state from their embassies and hotels to Buckingham Palace. Here, on the eve of the Coronation, The King hosted a lunch for the Governors-General and Prime Ministers of the 15 Commonwealth nations that recognise King Charles III as their monarch, including Australia and Canada. In the afternoon, The King and The Prince and Princess of Wales made a surprise appearance to greet well-wishers who had gathered on The Mall before attending a reception at Marlborough House, seat of the Commonwealth Secretariat, for leaders from the Commonwealth of Nations, the voluntary association of 56 countries of which The King is also the Head. Rounding off a busy day, The King then joined world leaders and royalty representing 203 countries for a final glittering reception.

Coronation Day itself began early for all those involved. At the Royal Mews, the grooms exercised the horses and then settled them down before they faced the excitement of the crowds. The coaches were given a final polish and uniforms were inspected, the horses were groomed and their tails set neatly in bandages before they were harnessed and saddled.

In the Abbey, the first guests took their seats at 7.30am, with heads of state, former prime ministers and members of the Royal Family arriving from 9.30am. The Dean and Canons prepared the regalia for the ceremony by carrying the two crowns, the Orb, sceptres, ring and Armills in procession from the Jerusalem Chamber to the High Altar. The consecrated oil for the Anointing was placed in the Ampulla and left on the altar with the Coronation Spoon while the Imperial State Crown was placed on the altar in St Edward the Confessor's chapel.

PREVIOUS PAGE:
The Diamond Jubilee State Coach conveying The King and Queen to Westminster Abbey on Coronation Day.

OPPOSITE:
Scenes from the rehearsal which took place between midnight and 3am on Wednesday 3 May 2023 as thousands of soldiers on foot and on horseback marched from Buckingham Palace to Westminster Abbey in preparation for the real event. Musical instruments were carried by members of the various military bands but to avoid disturbing sleeping residents only the drums were played to keep the soldiers marching in time.

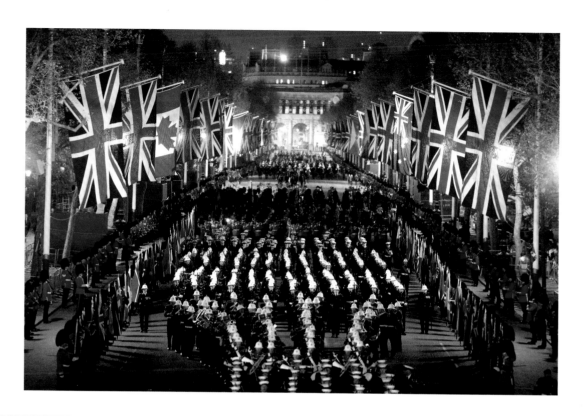

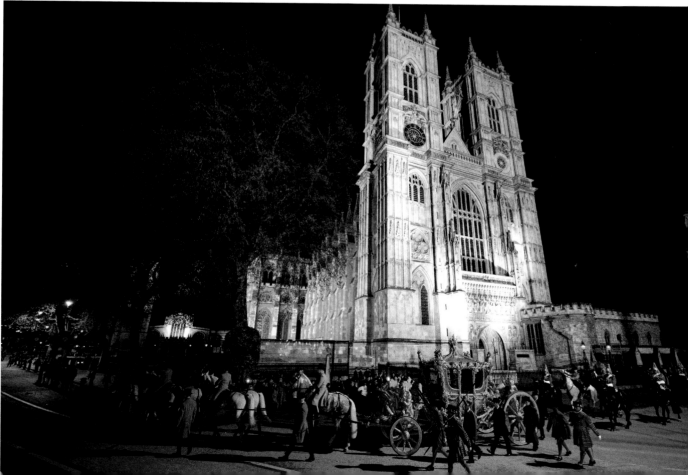

The Procession to the Abbey

THE KING AND QUEEN TRAVELLED to Westminster Abbey in the Diamond Jubilee State Coach. This carriage is the most modern of the horse-drawn vehicles in the Royal Mews. Made in Australia to commemorate Queen Elizabeth II's Diamond Jubilee in 2012, it combines traditional design with modern suspension. The body is made of aluminium, and six hydraulic stabilisers prevent the coach from swaying. The coach is topped by a crown made of oak taken from HMS *Victory*, the flagship of Admiral Lord Nelson. The crown itself is hollowed out, leaving space for a camera to be inserted offering a 'carriage-eye' view of the procession.

The interior of the coach is furnished with objects and materials from places and items with royal and historical associations. The handrails are made from timber from the Royal Yacht *Britannia* while the window frames and panelling include wood from Caernarfon Castle, Canterbury Cathedral, the *Mary Rose* (Henry VIII's flagship), Captain Cook's ship HMS *Endeavour*, 10 Downing Street and the Antarctic bases of Captain Scott and Sir Ernest Shackleton. In addition, the interior incorporates a fragment of the Stone of Destiny donated by the Scottish Government (see page 52) and a British lead musket ball from the battlefield at Waterloo.

As The King and Queen passed through the Centre Gate at Buckingham Palace to proceed down The Mall, they were accompanied on their route to Westminster Abbey by 200 troops of the Sovereign's Escort of the Household Cavalry. The procession passed through Admiralty Arch and the south-eastern side of Trafalgar Square before travelling down Whitehall and around Parliament Square to Broad Sanctuary, and arriving at the Abbey, where the Coronation Service began at 11 o'clock precisely.

OPPOSITE:
The King and Queen begin their historic journey to Westminster Abbey in the Diamond Jubilee State Coach.
    Seamus the Irish wolfhound, the regimental mascot of the Irish Guards, played a prominent role in the Coronation parade, briefly stealing the show to the delight of the watching crowds.

The Order of Service

OPPOSITE:
An illuminated page from the 14th-century manuscript, the *Liber Regalis*, depicting the act of crowning an unidentified monarch.

BELOW:
The Order of Service for the Coronation ceremony.

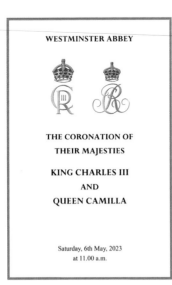

WESTMINSTER ABBEY

THE CORONATION OF
THEIR MAJESTIES

KING CHARLES III
AND
QUEEN CAMILLA

Saturday, 6th May, 2023
at 11.00 a.m.

THE CEREMONY USED FOR THE CORONATION of Their Majesties King Charles III and Queen Camilla was based on instructions recorded in the *Liber Regalis* ('Royal Book'), a 14th-century illuminated manuscript held in Westminster Abbey. Historians think it incorporates elements of ritual dating back to the 10th century that were passed on orally and only written down in the Middle Ages.

The *Liber Regalis* describes the main parts of the service, combining the solemnity of a religious ritual with orchestrated pageantry to legitimise the authority of the new ruler. First comes the Procession and Recognition, when the new monarch is presented to the congregation and greeted with the words: 'God Save King Charles!', a rite with its roots in Parliament's Anglo-Saxon predecessor, the 'witan', or gathering of nobles. The Coronation Oath that follows is the only legal aspect of the ceremony, confirming the contract between the monarch and the people.

The holiest part of the ceremony is the Anointing of the Sovereign by the Archbishop of Canterbury, the Church of England's senior cleric. It is followed by the Investiture, in which the new monarch is presented with the various symbols of kingship. The culmination of the ceremony is the Crowning, which is followed by the Enthroning and the feudal ritual of the Homage. In the past, the Archbishops, Bishops and all the peers of the realm would pledge loyalty to the new monarch. This part of the service was simplified in the Coronation of May 2023 and only the Archbishop of Canterbury and The Prince of Wales paid homage to The King (see page 100).

While the order of the coronation set out in the *Liber Regalis* is followed, there is always scope to adapt the ceremony. In May 2023, the Coronation of Charles III reflected The King's many personal interests in sustainability, diversity and inclusivity – whilst also being rooted in the ancient rituals of kingship.

The Procession and Recognition

I N A CONTRAST TO PREVIOUS CORONATIONS, the Coronation Procession through the nave and choir was an opportunity for inclusivity and diversity that was one of the key themes of the ceremony. One of the elements of this Coronation that reflected The King's longstanding respect for people of all religions was his commitment to 'foster an environment in which people of all faiths and beliefs may live freely'. Hence the Coronation Procession through the nave of the Abbey and up to the Coronation Theatre was led for the first time by religious leaders representing the Buddhist, Hindu, Jewish, Muslim and Sikh faiths.

Next in the procession were representatives from His Majesty's Realms carrying their national flags, accompanied by their Governors-General and Prime Ministers, followed by the Coronation Choir.

Last to reach the Coronation Theatre were The King and Queen, where The King was greeted by 14-year-old Samuel Strachan, the longest-serving chorister of the Chapel Royal, St James's Palace, with the words: 'Your Majesty, as children of the Kingdom of God we welcome you in the name of the King of Kings', to which The King replied: 'In His name and after His example I come not to be served but to serve'.

After a moment of silent prayer, the Archbishop of Canterbury greeted the congregation who then heard Sir Bryn Terfel sing the Kyrie ('Lord have Mercy, Christ have Mercy') in Welsh ('Arglwydd, trugarhâ'), marking the first use of the Welsh language at a coronation and symbolising The King's 64 years and 44 days as Prince of Wales (from 1958 to 2022).

The Recognition followed, whereby His Majesty faced the congregation while the Archbishop of Canterbury said: 'I here present unto you King Charles, your undoubted King: Wherefore all you who are come this day to do your homage and service: are you willing to do the same?', to which all replied in unison, 'God save King Charles'. The same words were repeated by Lady Angiolini, a Lady of the Thistle, and Baroness Amos, a Lady of the Garter – members of the oldest orders of chivalry in Scotland and England respectively – and Christopher Finney, GC, Chair of the Victoria Cross and George Cross Association – the highest military and civil honours awarded by the monarch for valour and heroism.

The Coronation Oath

I N THE NEXT PART OF THE CEREMONY, The King was presented with a newly bound copy of the Bible by the Moderator (Chair) of the General Assembly of the Church of Scotland, who announced that the Gospels serve 'as the rule for the whole life and government of Christian princes'. As he knelt and placed his right hand on the Bible, The King was asked to commit himself to exercise justice and mercy in his judgements, to respect the laws and customs of the Peoples of the United Kingdom of Great Britain and Northern Ireland and the Realms and Territories that recognise him as monarch; and to declare himself to be a faithful Protestant, committed to maintaining and preserving the Church of England, its bishops and clergy and the churches committed to their charge.

Monarchs have been required to take the Oath as part of the coronation ceremony since 1689, when the Catholic monarch James II was removed from the throne in what has gone down in history as the Glorious, or the Bloodless, Revolution, to be replaced by the Protestant Queen Mary II and King William III. Having promised to uphold and maintain the said enactments 'to the best of my powers', the King kissed the Bible and signed the written Oath with a pen made especially for the occasion.

In the sermon that followed, the Archbishop of Canterbury emphasised that 'with the privilege of power comes the duty to serve'. He said that the people who had gathered at the Abbey to witness the Coronation represented the many people around the world who work with charities and build a sense of community, and he paid tribute to The King's charitable work caring for the vulnerable, nurturing and encouraging the young and conserving the natural world.

Once again Welsh was heard in the plainsong chant, 'Veni Creator Spiritus', that followed, with verses also being sung in Scots Gaelic and Irish Gaelic.

OPPOSITE:
King Charles III places his hands on the Bible to swear the Coronation Oath required of him by a Parliamentary Act dating from 1689.

BELOW:
The King is required to sign two copies of the Oath in the presence of witnesses; one goes to the Court of Session in Edinburgh and the other is preserved in the Privy Council Register.

The Anointing

THE ANOINTING IS THE MOST SACRED and religiously significant part of the Coronation Service, the ritual through which the monarch is considered to have been consecrated by God for the duties of a sovereign. For this part of the ceremony, The King's Robe of State was removed along with all the other trappings of kingship. Wearing a plain white gown symbolising purity and humility, The King moved to sit in the Coronation Chair for his Anointing.

The Anointing establishes a direct connection between the monarch and the divine, and is a moment so sacred that it is concealed from public view. As was the case in 1953, it was the only part of the Coronation not to be televised. The screen used on this occasion consisted of an embroidered cloth suspended from a wooden frame. The four oak poles of the screen were made from a windblown oak from the Windsor estate, planted in 1765. Gilded bronze eagles were mounted on the front two poles, similar in form to the Ampulla used to contain the anointing oil used in this part of the ceremony. The embroidery on the cloth of the screen was inspired by the stained-glass window in the Chapel Royal at St James's Palace created for the late Queen's Golden Jubilee in 2002. The window and the Anointing Screen both feature the names of the Commonwealth nations set as leaves on a tree. The tree on the screen is also inhabited by birds and angels representing harmony and joy. The designer, Aiden Hart, said that the maroon, gold, blue and red colours of the embroidery were chosen to reflect the colours of the Cosmati mosaic pavement decorating the floor in front of the High Altar at Westminster Abbey, laid down in 1286 during the reign of Henry III.

The Chrism oil used to anoint His Majesty was consecrated in the Church of the Holy Sepulchre in Jerusalem on 3 March 2023. Based on a formula used at coronations for hundreds of years, the oil was created from olives harvested from two groves on the Mount of Olives, and perfumed with orange blossom and essential oils, including sesame, rose, jasmine, cinnamon, neroli, benzoin and amber.

The oil was poured from the Ampulla into the Coronation Spoon (see page 68) and used by the Archbishop of Canterbury to anoint The King on the hands, breast and forehead. During this most holy part of the service, the choir sang the traditional anthem, 'Zadok the Priest'. The words, from the first Book of Kings, have been used at every coronation since King Edgar's in AD 973 and the musical setting, by Handel, has been used since the coronation of George II in 1727.

TOP:
The King and Queen visited the Royal School of Needlework in March 2023, to see the embroidery of the Anointing Screen in progress and to meet the many craft-workers and embroiderers who contributed to the project.

BOTTOM:
The Anointing Screen in the Chapel Royal at St James's Palace in front of the stained-glass east window that inspired the embroidery. Both take the form of a tree with many branches and leaves decorated with the names of the Commonwealth nations.

The Investiture

A FTER THE ANOINTING, THE SCREEN was removed and The King knelt in front of the High Altar where the Archbishop of Canterbury prayed that he might 'govern and preserve the peoples committed to your charge in wealth, peace, and godliness'. The King then rose and was dressed in a series of traditional garments in preparation for the Investiture. First, he put on the white linen shift-like tunic intended to represent a priest's alb, known as the Colobium Sindonis. Over this was then placed the Supertunica (see page 56). Made for the coronation of King George V but to a design that has changed little since medieval coronations, the Supertunica echoes priestly robes and is a reminder of the divine nature of kingship. It was fastened with the Girdle worn at the coronation of King George VI in 1937.

Returning to the Coronation Chair, The King was presented with the chivalric symbols of the Spurs and the magnificent Jewelled Sword of Offering, before being presented with the Armills, or bracelets of wisdom and sincerity. Next, the Stole Royal, a long band of embroidered silk, commissioned by the Worshipful Company of Girdlers, was presented by The Prince of Wales and draped around The King's neck. This was the only new garment to be made especially for The King's Coronation. Designed by the College of Arms and embroidered by the Royal School of Needlework, it incorporates a Tudor crown, rose, thistle, leek and shamrock, a dove to represent the Holy Spirit, the keys of St Peter and the symbols of various saints.

The King was then dressed in the Imperial Mantle or Robe Royal. Made for George IV in 1821, the Mantle is a flowing cloak made of cloth of gold and woven with coloured threads in a pattern of foliage, crowns and fleurs-de-lis with roses, thistles and shamrocks.

Last to be presented were the Sovereign's Orb and the Coronation Ring, which, along with all the other regalia, were returned to the altar. Finally, The King donned the Coronation Glove on his right hand and was presented with the Sovereign's Sceptre with Cross, representing temporal power, and the Sovereign's Sceptre with Dove as a token of the importance of justice and mercy in the exercise of power.

The Coronation Ring is brought from the High Altar and presented to The King by The Right Honourable The Lord Patel of Bradford. Baron Patel was one of four peers selected to represent all 778 members of the House of Lords.

The Crowning

The Most Reverend and Right Honourable Justin Welby, Lord Archbishop of Canterbury, Primate of All England and Metropolitan, raises St Edward's Crown before placing it upon The King's head.

THE CULMINATION OF THE CEREMONY is the moment of crowning itself. Robed and seated on the Coronation Chair, and holding the two Sceptres, The King waited for the congregation to stand as the Dean of Westminster brought forward St Edward's Crown and handed it to the Archbishop of Canterbury. Lifting the Crown, the Archbishop said the prayer of blessing before placing it on The King's head and standing back to cry 'God save The King!'. The guests in the Abbey responded 'God Save The King!' and a fanfare by Richard Strauss was sounded.

Their acclamation was followed immediately by the pealing of the Abbey bells which rang out for two minutes in a joyful message to the nation, followed by a fanfare and the firing of a gun salute by The King's Troop, Royal Horse Artillery, stationed at Horse Guards Parade. This was the signal for guns to be fired at saluting stations across the UK, in overseas territories and on His Majesty's ships at sea. The salute in Horse Guards Parade took the form of a six-gun salvo (when all the guns are fired simultaneously) using howitzer guns that first saw service in the First World War. They were later modified for use as anti-aircraft guns in the Second World War.

Among the many other saluting stations that were fired in honour of the Coronation was the one that took place near Stonehenge. The Neolithic stone circle stood at the heart of the world's largest military camp during the First World War. One million soldiers from across the Commonwealth trained there between 1914 and 1918.

The Enthroning and the Homage

SIX CHURCH LEADERS THEN BLESSED The King – namely the Anglican Archbishops of Canterbury and York, the Greek Orthodox Archbishop of Thyateira and Great Britain, the Moderator of the Free Churches Group and the General Secretary of Churches Together in England (which collectively include most of the Christian congregations in England and Wales) and the Catholic Cardinal Archbishop of Westminster. Next, still wearing St Edward's Crown, The King left the ancient Coronation Chair and moved to the Throne Chair. Once newly built for each coronation, the Throne used for King Charles III was the same one that was made for his grandfather, King George VI, in 1937, newly refurbished for this occasion. As before, it was set in the main part of the Theatre where The King could be seen by the people and receive their homage.

Until 1902 every peer took his turn to pledge his loyalty in a ritual that dated back to the feudal period, when monarchs relied on the oaths of loyalty sworn at their coronations to keep their more powerful nobles in check. After 1902, however, homage was only undertaken by the senior peer in each rank of the peerage – dukes, marquesses, earls, viscounts and barons – a decision that saved a good deal of time. In 2023, the number of dignitaries paying official homage was reduced to just three: the Archbishop of Canterbury, Justin Welby, on behalf of the Church of England, The Prince of Wales and the Archbishop of Canterbury again, on behalf of 'all persons of goodwill'. All who so desired were then invited to swear allegiance to His Majesty and his heirs and successors.

The Prince of Wales, heir apparent to the throne in the traditional order of succession, pays homage to his father, the newly crowned King.

The Coronation of Queen Camilla

ONCE THE CORONATION OF THE KING had been completed, The Queen was blessed, anointed and crowned by the Archbishop of Canterbury in a simpler version of the same ceremony. Her Coronation ended with her enthronement alongside The King and the performance of the celebratory anthem 'Make A Joyful Noise'. Composed by Andrew Lloyd Webber for the occasion, this was an opportunity for glorious trumpets, drums and cymbal clashes giving musical form to the words of Psalm 98: 'O make a joyful noise unto the Lord all the earth. Sing unto the Lord with harp and the voice of a psalm. With trumpets and sound of cornet make a joyful noise before the Lord'.

Next came Communion, the central act of Christian worship, responding to the invitation of Jesus to his followers at the Last Supper to share bread and wine 'in remembrance of me'. After taking communion, The King and Queen left the Theatre and withdrew to St Edward's Chapel. Here The King was disrobed: the Imperial Mantle, Supertunica and Colobium Sindonis were removed, and he put on instead the impressive Robe of Estate (see page 56). Just as sumptuous as the Robe of State worn in the procession into the Abbey, the Robe of Estate is made of purple silk velvet and includes an elaborate ermine cape. St Edward's Crown was exchanged for the lighter Imperial State Crown, while The Queen also wore a Robe of Estate newly made by Ede & Ravenscroft and featuring embroidery by the Royal School of Needlework.

Intended as a celebration of Her Majesty's dedication to serving the nation, the Robe was created using traditional techniques with a contemporary design that reflects today's monarchy and draws upon The Queen's love of gardening, nature and the environment.

Carefully chosen to match The King's Robe of Estate, the rich purple velvet was embroidered by hand, using goldwork, a technique using metal threads dating back more than a thousand years. The Queen's 'CR' cypher featured prominently, along with a border of entwined roses, shamrock, thistle and daffodils, the emblematic flowers of the four nations of the UK. Altogether, the Robe incorporated 24 embroidered plants, many of them chosen for their personal association with The Queen, including Lily of the Valley, which was in Her Majesty's wedding bouquet; delphinium (also known as larkspur), which flowers in July, her birthday month; and scabious, also known as pincushion flowers, a reference to the Royal School of Needlework of which Her Majesty has been patron since 2017.

The Queen is crowned by the Archbishop of Canterbury using the crown of Queen Mary (see page 80).

The Coronation Procession

Accompanying the Gold State Coach
along The Mall are representatives of
the armed forces of Commonwealth
nations whose flags are borne (below)
by soldiers of the Grenadier Guards.

RETRACING THE ROUTE THEY TOOK to reach the Abbey, The King and Queen now returned to Buckingham Place along streets lined with cheering well-wishers, whose high spirits were not dampened by the day's wet weather. The royal couple, travelling in the Gold State Coach, were chaperoned by 4,000 Armed Forces personnel from across the UK joined by 400 from 40 Commonwealth countries and overseas territories – the largest military procession seen in London for many decades.

Eight processional groups took part in the parade, stepping in rhythm and keeping time to the pounding beats of 19 different bands all playing the same tune, though separated by a distance of more than a mile.

The mounted troops of the Household Cavalry, the senior armed service, led the procession, accompanied by The King's Troop, Royal Horse Artillery. Next came troops from across the Commonwealth, from Antigua to Zambia, creating a kaleidoscopic array of colourful uniforms, flanked by bearers carrying the flags of the Commonwealth and overseas territories. The Royal Air Force and members of the Royal Armoured Corps made up the third and fourth groups, then the Army's Corps and Infantry, including Gurkha riflemen from Nepal and grey beret-wearing Rangers from the army's newest regiment.

The sixth group included members of the Honourable Artillery Company, the British Army's oldest regiment, tracing its history back to incorporation in 1537. Members of the Royal Navy made up the seventh group, then the heads of the Army, Navy and Air Force and members of the Household Division.

Eight magnificent grey horses pulled the Gold State Coach carrying The King and Queen, flanked by various bodyguards, including four cavalrymen from the Royal Canadian Mounted Police in scarlet tunics and trade-mark brown felt hats. Close by, the Princess Royal followed on horseback in her role as Gold Stick in Waiting – the King's personal bodyguard – and another royal carriage conveyed The Prince and Princess of Wales, Prince George, Princess Charlotte and Prince Louis back to Buckingham Palace. Further carriages and cars from the Royal Mews transported The Duke and Duchess of Edinburgh, Lady Louise Mountbatten-Windsor and the Earl of Wessex, The Duke and Duchess of Gloucester, The Duke of Kent and Princess Alexandra.

The Buckingham Palace Balcony

O N ARRIVAL AT THE PALACE, The King and Queen made their way to the West Terrace, overlooking the gardens, to thank the troops involved in the Procession, who were ordered to present arms in a formal royal salute, then to 'remove headdress' and give three cheers for The King and Queen.

But for the crowds gathered at the gates of Buckingham Palace, there was just one more highlight to come: the appearance of the newly crowned King and Queen and other members of the Royal Family on the balcony to watch the Coronation Flypast. This had been planned as a display of six minutes involving the aircraft of all three armed services but low cloud meant that the plan had to be curtailed; instead, the display lasted for around two-and-a-half minutes and involved helicopters from the three services and a Red Arrows display team trailing red, white and blue smoke from their Hawk jets as they passed over the crowds.

The newly crowned King and Queen appeared together on the balcony at Buckingham Palace, having previously been joined by other members of the Royal Family to watch the Red Arrows formation team streaming red, white and blue plumes made of environmentally friendly dye colours.

The Coronation Weekend

THE CORONATION WAS WATCHED by millions in the UK and around the world. Large crowds travelled to London to see the processions to and from Westminster Abbey in person, while big screens were erected at more than 30 locations around the country to enable people in the UK's larger towns and cities to watch the ceremony.

The celebrations continued over the Bank Holiday weekend. On Sunday 7 May, vast numbers took part in street parties co-ordinated by the Big Lunch charity. The Queen is the charity's patron, which has been encouraging people to make community lunches an annual occasion since 2009. This year's Coronation-themed event was marked by more than 67,000 parties as community groups across the nation gathered in streets, gardens, parks and community spaces to share friendship, food and fun.

Several members of the Royal Family took part: The Duke and Duchess of Edinburgh attended a Big Lunch at Cranleigh in Surrey, The Princess Royal and Vice Admiral Sir Timothy Laurence visited a community street party in Swindon and Princesses Beatrice and Eugenie took part in one in Chalfont St Giles in Buckinghamshire. The Coronation Big Lunch at Morecambe Bay set a new record for the scale of its picnic, with 900 tables laid out along the 1.5km-long promenade.

The same evening a special Coronation Concert took place on the East Lawn of Windsor Castle. Broadcast by the BBC, the concert brought together an international cast of entertainers, including American singers Lionel Ritchie and Katy Perry, Italian opera star Andrea Bocelli and Welsh bass-baritone Sir Bryn Terfel.

Watched by millions on television screens around the world and by a live audience of 20,000 in the grounds of Windsor Castle, the Coronation Concert on Sunday 7 May 2023 included a performance by Katy Perry who sang two of her most popular songs, 'Roar' and 'Firework'.

Across the country and the Commonwealth, activities were planned by friends, families and communities throughout the Coronation weekend. From sheep races to street parties, parades to light displays, from flower shows to fun runs and fancy-dress parties, people found their own ways to mark the historic occasion.

On the Bank Holiday Monday, the focus remained on community, as The Big Help Out encouraged people to try volunteering and come together to support their own communities in the hope of creating a lasting legacy from the Coronation weekend.

Setting an example, The Prince and Princess of Wales (who is joint President of the Scouts) joined other volunteers in Slough to renovate the 3rd Upton Scouts' hut; The Duchess of Edinburgh took part in a puppy training session in Reading run by the Guide Dogs for the Blind Association, while the Prime Minister, Rishi Sunak, served lunch at the Mill End Community Centre in Rickmansworth, Hertfordshire.

Fans entering into the spirit of the Coronation after gathering in their thousands on the historic day having waited for hours for a prime spot along The Mall and refusing to have their high spirits dampened by the Coronation Day rain.

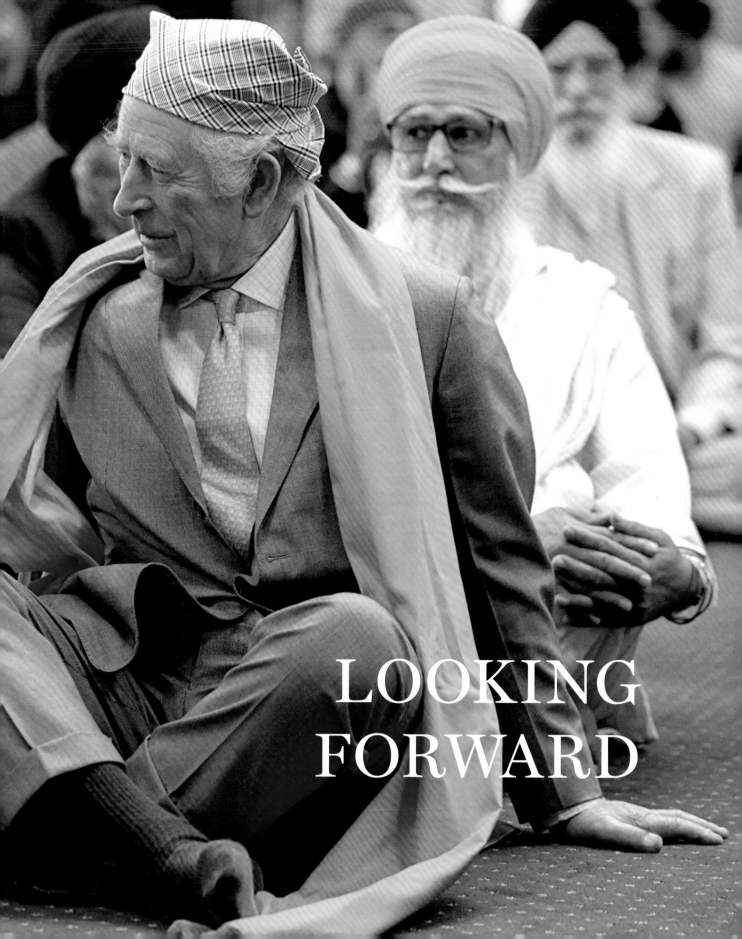

LOOKING
FORWARD

Looking Forward

King Charles has promised to be the 'protector of faiths' and he gave substance to this promise when he attended prayers to inaugurate the newly built Guru Nanak Gurdwara in Luton on 12 December 2022.

Working members of the Royal Family are patrons of hundreds of charities, representing their particular passions and interests. When the then Duke of Cambridge took to the streets to sell copies of *The Big Issue* on 22 June 2022 he said that ending homelessness was a cause close to his heart and he paid tribute to the compassionate volunteers who worked tirelessly to support the vulnerable. Her Majesty The Queen has a long-standing interest in encouraging children to read, believing that literacy encourages greater aspiration and a rich imaginative life. Here she is shown visiting the Coram Beanstalk charity where trained volunteers help children build their reading skills and self-confidence. The Princess of Wales shares The Queen's interest in childhood development and campaigns for increased public understanding of the crucial importance of the first five years of a child's life in developing into a happy and healthy adult.

THE MONTHS BETWEEN the Accession and the Coronation were a time of national change as the country adjusted from the longest-serving monarch in British history to its first king for more than 70 years. The seamless transition from one sovereign to another demonstrated the strength and continuity of the British monarchy. Their Majesties King Charles and Queen Camilla were able to draw on the traditions of the past to set the tone for their reign, one that not only reflects their commitment to the same dedication and duty that defined the reign of Queen Elizabeth II but also looks forward to a renewed spirit of community and public service, and to a resurgence of the values of friendship and fairness, of diversity, tolerance and mutual respect. 'By listening to each other', His Majesty has said, 'we will find so many of the solutions that we seek.'

In his declaration at the first Privy Council meeting of his reign, The King promised to follow the late Queen's inspiring example, dedicating himself, as she had done, to the peace, harmony and prosperity of people everywhere. Succeeding Her late Majesty as Head of the Commonwealth, The King committed himself, too, to its values of 'peace and justice, tolerance, respect and solidarity; care for our environment and for the most vulnerable among us'.

The death of Queen Elizabeth II provoked an outpouring of emotion across the country, which was unified behind The King as he led the mourning for a beloved Sovereign. The succeeding months marked the beginning of a new era, culminating in the historic Coronation of Their Majesties King Charles III and Queen Camilla, as the country came together again in May 2023 to celebrate the making – and crowning – of its new monarch.

The Foundling Hospital moved i
from this site in 1926 and chan
mmunity support for children
y known as Coram. Our mis
rk to create better chance
f their rights and welfa

Acknowledgements

We are grateful to His Majesty The King for permission to produce this book and to use extracts from his various speeches.

We are also grateful to Ede & Ravenscroft, Ben Fitzpatrick, Mappin & Webb, Bruce Oldfield, the Royal Mews, the Royal School of Needlework and the Canons and Dean and Chapter of Westminster Abbey for their help in allowing photographs to be taken or supplying reference material for use in this book.

Thanks are due to the following Royal Household colleagues for helping with the compilation of this book: Aaminah Akram, Katie Buckhalter, Amanda Foster, Sally Goodsir, Caroline de Guitaut, Kathryn Jones, Tim Knox, Karen Lawson, Iain Lewis, Daniel Partridge, Alexander Scully and Dee Vianna.

All images are Royal Collection Trust / © His Majesty King Charles III 2023 unless otherwise indicated below.

Royal Collection Trust is grateful to the following for permission to use their copyright material in this book:

Royal Collection Trust / © His Majesty King Charles III 2023. Photographer: Mappin & Webb: pp. 62 (top left), 66, 78, 81
Royal Collection Trust / © His Majesty King Charles III 2023. With thanks to the Dean and Canons of Westminster Abbey: p. 53 (top right)
The Governor and Company of the Bank of England: p. 36 (bank notes)
Hugo Burnand / Royal Household 2023: pp. 4, 33, 35, 57, 59
Ede & Ravenscroft: pp. 62 (below left; below centre), 63 (top right; below right)
Getty Images: pp. 25, 93, 101, 114/15, 117 (below)
Kensington Palace: p. 117 (top right)
Johnny Millar (www.johnnymillar.com): pp. 30/1
PA / Alamy: pp. 2, 6/7, 8, 9, 11, 13, 14, 15, 16, 17, 18, 19, 20, 21, 23, 26, 27, 28, 29, 32, 34, 37, 39, 40, 41, 43, 45, 47, 48/9, 51, 53 (top left; below), 54, 55, 64/5, 68, 70 (right), 74 (below), 82/3, 85, 91, 92, 95, 97, 99, 103, 104, 105 (top), 108, 109, 110, 111, 112 (left), 119
Ruth Park-Pearson: p. 46
Andy Parsons: p. 117 (top left)
Royal Mail Group Ltd 2023: p. 36 (stamp)
The Royal Mint Limited 2022: p. 36 (coin)
Royal School of Needlework: pp. 56, 58 (top)
Dean and Chapter of Westminster Abbey: p. 89

Every effort has been made to trace and credit all known copyright or reproduction rights holders; the publishers apologise for any errors or omissions and welcome these being brought to their attention.

OPPOSITE:
In the final moments of the Coronation ceremony the Westminster Abbey choir sang Andrew Lloyd Webber's anthem, 'Make A Joyful Noise'. Copies of the anthem were then distributed to thousands of churches around the country for performance on the following day.

Published 2023 by Royal Collection Trust
York House
St James's Palace
London SW1A 1BQ

ISBN 978 1 909741 88 1
103439

10 9 8 7 6 5 4 3 2 1

A catalogue record for this book is available from the British Library.

Publisher: Kate Owen
Project Manager: Polly Fellows
Text: Kate Owen, Pamela Hartshorne and Polly Fellows
Designed by Adrian Hunt
Production Management by Sarah Tucker
Typeset in Miller and Foundry Sterling
Colour reproduction by Alta Image, London
Printed on Claro silk 150gsm
Printed and bound in Wales by Gomer Press

www.carbonbalancedprint.com
CBP2275

Jacket illustrations

FRONT:
The Official Coronation Portrait of His Majesty King Charles III
(© Hugo Burnand / Royal Household 2023)

BACK:
The King and Queen greet well-wishers from the balcony of
Buckingham Palace (© PA / Alamy)